Who On Earth is Archie Carr?

Protector of Sea Turtles

Read about other Scientists
Saving the Earth

Who on Earth is Aldo Leopold?
Father of Wildlife Ecology
ISBN: 978-1-59845-115-3
ISBN: 1-59845-115-4

Who on Earth is Dian Fossey?
Defender of the Mountain Gorillas
ISBN: 978-1-59845-117-7
ISBN: 1-59845-117-0

Who on Earth is Jane Goodall?
Champion for the Chimpanzees
ISBN: 978-1-59845-119-1
ISBN: 1-59845-119-7

Who on Earth is Rachel Carson?
Mother of the Environmental Movement
ISBN: 978-1-59845-116-0
ISBN: 1-59845-116-2

Who on Earth is Sylvia Earle?
Undersea Explorer of the Ocean
ISBN: 978-1-59845-118-4
ISBN: 1-59845-118-9

Who On Earth is Archie Carr?

Protector of Sea Turtles

Christine Webster

Enslow Publishers, Inc.
40 Industrial Road
Box 398
Berkeley Heights, NJ 07922
USA

http://www.enslow.com

Library of Congress Cataloging-in-Publication Data

Webster, Christine.
  Who on earth is Archie Carr? : protector of sea turtles / Christine Webster.
    p. cm. — (Scientists saving the earth)
  Includes bibliographical references and index.
  Summary: "Details Archie Carr's life, with chapters devoted to his early years, life, work, writings, and lasting contributions"—Provided by publisher.
  ISBN-13: 978-1-59845-120-7
  ISBN-10: 1-59845-120-0
  1. Carr, Archie Fairly, 1909 –1987—Juvenile literature. 2. Herpetologists—United States—Biography—Juvenile literature. 3. Sea turtles—Juvenile literature. I. Title.
  QL31.C34W43 2009
  597.9092—dc22
  [B]
                                    2008032016
Printed in the United States of America

10 9 8 7 6 5 4 3 2 1

To Our Readers:
We have done our best to make sure all Internet Addresses in this book were active and appropriate when we went to press. However, the author and the publisher have no control over and assume no liability for the material available on those Internet sites or on other Web sites they may link to. Any comments or suggestions can be sent by e-mail to comments@enslow.com or to the address on the back cover.

♻ Enslow Publishers, Inc., is committed to printing our books on recycled paper. The paper in every book contains 10% to 30% post-consumer waste (PCW). The cover board on the outside of each book contains 100% PCW. Our goal is to do our part to help young people and the environment too!

Photo Credits: © Allan Cressler, p. 30; © Caribbean Conservation Corporation (CCC), p. 89; Courtesy of the Department of Special and Area Studies Collections, George A. Smathers Libraries, University of Florida, p.35; Courtesy of Mimi Carr. pp. 12, 16, 24, 32, 33; © David Kirk. p. 19; © Enslow Publishers, Inc, p. 11; © Kevin G. W. Olson, p. 93; © National Biological Information Infrastructure, p. 38; National Park Service: Padre Island National Seashore, pp. 39, 49 (top), 58; © National Oceanographic and Atmospheric Administration (NOAA), pp. 41, 45, 47, 51 (bottom), 53, 56, 65 (Photo: Michael P. Jensen), 68, 82; © Shutterstock, pp. 6–7, 22; © Time & Life Pictures/Getty Images, p. 27; © United States Fish and Wildlife Service, pp. 73, 78–79, 84, 94, 96; © Ursula Keuper-Bennett and Peter Bennett, p. 71; © William D. Bachman / Photo Researchers, Inc., pp. 62–63

Cover Photo: Archie Carr portrait with binoculars, 1961 Credit: George A. Smathers Libraries, University of Florida, Special and Area Studies Collections

Contents

Hawksbill turtle

Introduction

Ayoung boy lounges on an old dock in the blistering sun. His fishing line silently bobs up and down in the murky waters. The heat is so comforting that he fights sleep. His eyes grow heavier and heavier. Soon, sleep comes over him.

By the dock, the water's surface is broken. A tiny nose pokes up and blows out, curiously staring at the sleeping figure. Its body rises upward toward the water's surface. Its shell now basking in the heat of the sun. In his drowsy state, the boy senses that he is not alone. Lazily, he opens one eye. A pair of dark eyes is staring back at him from the murky waters.

It's a turtle! Suddenly wide awake, the boy drops his fishing rod and slides onto his stomach. Face-to-face, the turtle and the boy quietly study each other. The boy is fascinated. He smiles at the turtle's old and wise-looking face. But in a flash it is over. The turtle ducks his head into the waters and swims away from the dock.

The boy is unaware that this encounter will change his life forever. Or that it will shape his entire future. Each summer, the boy will return to the old dock to catch a glimpse of the turtle. The boy's name was Archie Carr.

This summer was the beginning of a lifelong journey—a journey about the plight of the marine turtle. From that very first face-to-face meeting with a marine turtle, Archie Carr will dedicate the rest of his life to study of this species. He will educate himself on marine turtles. He will pass his knowledge on to others about marine turtles. He will protect the species and become an active conservationist of them. In fact, what is known today of marine turtles is because of Archie Carr. He is sometimes affectionately referred to as the "father of sea turtle research."[1]

One lonely summer day spent discovering a new creature actually inspired an entire life's work. Young Archie Carr thought he was just meeting a curious new friend that hot summer day. Instead, the experience helped him decide his future work—saving an entire species of marine turtle. Without Archie Carr, the marine turtle might not exist today.

Who Is Archie Carr?

Archie Fairly Carr, Jr., was born on June 16, 1909.[1] He was born in Mobile, Alabama, to Archie Carr, Sr., and Louise Gordon Deaderick. Archie Carr, Sr., had studied to become a pastor. He preached in local churches, moving his family from time to time when a new pastor was needed at a different church.

Archie Carr's mother had studied to become a classical pianist. Her dream was interrupted by a temporary paralysis in one of her arms.[2] Unfortunately, this ended her career as a classical pianist, and she became a piano teacher instead. She had a keen ear for music and a talent for teaching.

These gifts would later be passed on to her eldest son, Archie.

Besides preaching, the senior Carr loved to hunt and fish. He hunted because he enjoyed it, and because it was a means to bring food to the table. The senior Carr took his son hunting with him on many trips, which instilled a passion for hunting in Archie.[3] Together they would hunt on month-long trips in the woods. Sometimes they would camp as an entire family, hunting and fishing as part of the holiday fun.

Like his father, Archie loved nature and the outdoors. He had a fascination with the world around him. His father nurtured Archie's interest in nature. Even as a young boy this interest was apparent. Archie's favorite book was the *Jungle Book* by Rudyard Kipling.[4] The book was about a young boy raised in the jungle by animals.

In 1917, when Archie was just eight years old, his brother, Thomas Carr, was born. By this time, the family was living in Fort Worth, Texas. Archie's father was teaching at the local church.

Illustration from
The Jungle Book

Archie Carr is shown holding two turtles in 1919.

His mother was giving piano lessons. Archie spent his free time discovering nature. He loved collecting small animals. Reptiles and turtles had always fascinated him. In his backyard, he would hunt around for tiny animals to study. He kept a small collection of snakes, lizards, and little turtles in small cages and boxes. They were kept in his backyard.[5] Once he even caught an armadillo!

At a very young age, Archie was fascinated by turtles. He loved the look of a turtle's face. He was once quoted as saying, "I just like the look on their faces. There is an old, wise, sort of durable, aboriginal look about turtles that fascinates people."[6] Archie could study them for hours and never get tired of watching them.

Archie Carr, Sr., continued to hunt with his sons throughout their childhood. Sometimes he liked to take them camping beside rivers. They would choose different locations for their trips. Sometimes they would travel with other families. They would hunt for quail, turkeys, and deer.[7] Whatever was caught was never wasted. Archie's mother would cook the game for them to eat.

When Archie was eleven years old, the family moved again. His father was given a new church to preach at in Savannah, Georgia. This was the third church where Archie Carr, Sr., was the pastor.

It wasn't long after the family were settled in Savannah that Archie Carr, Sr., wanted to hunt again. This time he wanted a more permanent place to camp for vacations. He wanted a place where he could go away with his family and hunt and fish. He bought a cottage on the coast in Darien, Georgia.[8] Here he knew he could go away with his family. And he could take his boys fishing and hunting—exactly what he loved most. So each summer, the Carrs headed to the cottage in Darien for at least one month.

During the lazy summer days, Archie would fish off an old dock. One summer, a memorable thing happened to Archie. As he waited on the dock hoping for the fish to bite, he had an unexpected visitor: A huge loggerhead turtle swam up the creek to where he was fishing. Almost taunting him, it swam right up to Archie. Archie was very excited. He loved studying the turtle's face and watching it glide smoothly through the water. He even learned to recognize the markings on its shell.

Each summer, Archie couldn't wait to spot the turtle again. For six continuous years, Archie would look forward to seeing this same turtle return. Now, he could easily identify it. He was able to point out important details about the log-gerhead. He noted that this turtle was very big, more than five hundred pounds in weight.[9] He also knew that it had a patch of barnacles over one of its eyes. These observational skills were important and would remain with him throughout his life.

Growing Up

As a young teenager, Archie liked many activities. He continued to enjoy hunting and fishing. He still loved collecting small animals.[10] His backyard was filled with cages of snakes, lizards, and other animals.

But Archie wasn't just interested in nature. Archie also loved words. He loved listening to the sounds and rhythms of languages.[11] He loved the way words sounded off the tongue. He enjoyed reading the written word, and the way words were put together on paper. During school, he often tried out for various school plays. He even won leading roles as an actor.[12]

Archie also liked to have fun with his friends, and they often went out sailing together. It was common to find him gliding along the smooth water in a boat. But life wasn't all fun and games for Archie Carr.

He was a very hard worker. For instance, during one summer he worked as a stevedore on the local docks, loading and unloading cargo on ships.[13] It is very hard work. A stevedore must be strong. Archie Carr was not very big or strong. He was tall and lanky. Most local kids who were hired as stevedores found that the job was much too difficult. They usually quit after the first week, but Archie stuck it out.

⬆Archie Carr sitting with his parents, Archibald (Parson) and Mimi Carr in 1930.

As a stevedore, Archie got to appreciate his love of language even further. Many people who he worked with on the docks spoke Gullah.[14] It is a language that is spoken by ancestors of African-Americans who were brought to America as slaves. It is a sing-songy language spoken by African Americans living along the southeastern coast of Africa.

Not many other people could learn this difficult language. But Archie Carr had inherited his mother's musical ear. He easily picked up phrases and songs from the Gullah language. In later years, Archie was able to relate stories to his students, exactly the way they were told to him, in any language.[15]

Archie enjoyed his summer as a stevedore and learning another language. In fact, he loved language so much that he decided to study English at college.[16] He wanted to become an English teacher.

Unfortunately, Archie's college education had a bumpy start. When Archie was eighteen years old, he went on another fishing trip. During the trip, he developed osteomyelitis, an infection in his right arm. Osteomyelitis is an infectious inflamatory disease of the bone. The infection travels through the bloodstream to a part of bone. Eventually, the infection wears away the bone until the bone becomes soft. The softened bone eventually dies. Archie Carr became very sick from osteomyelitis.[17]

As a result, he had to have many operations, as the infection kept returning. In two years, Archie went through seven operations! During each operation, the doctors removed parts of the bone in his right arm. However, during the last operation, the doctors learned the infection had spread even further. It was now in his elbow joint. They had no choice but to immobilize his elbow joint. This would mean that Archie Carr would have no movement in his elbow. The doctors gave him a choice. He could either have his arm locked into a straight position, or he could decide to have it locked into a bent position. Either way, it would never move like a normal elbow joint again. Archie Carr chose to have his arm secured in a bent position. His reasoning was that he might still be able to hold a rifle with the arm in a bent position. This would enable him to continue his love of hunting.

There was another downside to all these operations. They had interrupted the start of his college education. Archie was forced to delay his college studies for those two years. After his final surgery, he went to Weaver College in North Carolina. Here he lived in one of the dormitories. One of his roommates was Cuban.[18] He spoke Spanish. Archie's fascination with language grew even further. Instead of having trouble understanding his roommate, Archie decided to learn the Spanish language.

His fascination with language grew even further. Archie picked up the Spanish language almost immediately from his roommate.[19] Eventually, Archie could even speak entirely in Spanish with him. Little did Archie Carr realize that being fluent in Spanish would help him in later years. It would make his future travels to Honduras and Costa Rica easier.

⬆ Dora Canal in Umatilla, Florida

The University of Florida

By 1930, Archie and Thomas Carr were on their way into adulthood. Their parents were thinking about their retirements. It was time to move once again. This time the Carr family traveled to Florida.

Archie Carr, Sr., was getting ready for semiretirement. He wanted to cut back on his work as a pastor, settle down, and not have to move his family anymore. He was careful in choosing where the family would live. He looked for an area that he knew everyone in his family would love. He chose a wilderness area that had more than fifteen hundred lakes. It was located in Umatilla, Florida.[20] It was the perfect place for the entire family. Archie could further his education at a nearby university and he was surrounded by a natural environment, an environment that he loved.

Archie transferred to the University of Florida where he planned to continue his education. He would continue his study of the English language. He wanted to become a teacher.[21] His professors could see that Archie loved language. They encouraged Archie to write. Although Archie would later go on to switch his major, studying English gave him a great tool. In fact, his gift for the written word would later lead Archie to write for various publications—combining his love of language with his love of nature.

During his studies at the university, Archie made a decision: He would switch his major. Instead of English, he decided he wanted to study biology. Biologists learn about various creatures, their origins, growth, reproduction, behavior, and characteristics. Archie had always loved small animals and reptiles. What better way to learn about animals than to study them. Imagine the things he could learn!

At first, Archie was going to take biology courses and become a herpetologist. A herpetologist studies reptiles and amphibians—exactly what Archie Carr had done his entire childhood. But at the University of Florida, Archie decided he was going to become a zoologist, instead, and study all species of animals. As a zoologist, he would not be limiting his study of animals in any way.

What changed his mind to study zoology and changed his focus from English? It was an ecology class. During this class, Archie was fascinated by the huge water hyacinth plants that had been brought in for study.[22] Inside these plants were lots of hidden discoveries, tiny unknown creatures. This made him realize that there were so many other amazing little things out in the world, waiting to be discovered. He said, "I realize one of the factors that influenced my decision was the

◔ A closeup of water hyacinths.

hyacinth fauna—the diverse assortment of self-effacing little animals that most people didn't even know existed."[23]

New species were just waiting to be discovered! Archie Carr knew that he wanted to be the one to discover them. He wanted to find and identify these creatures. He wanted to learn about them, and later protect them.

2

Student and Teacher

Switching to zoology was a good decision for Archie Carr. He would get to study reptiles, amphibians, and many other animals. He would learn how to identify them and classify them into groups.[1] He would also learn about their habitats and how animals have changed and evolved over the years. To evolve means to change and adapt to new lifestyles. Archie would write about these animals too, combining his love of nature along with his love of language.

Now Archie's love of "hunting" meant hunting to find things to study. He traveled all over Florida to find new specimens, as well as study those

Archie Carr went on a collecting trip in 1932.

already known. Nothing was off limits in his learning. If he discovered something new about a species, he would record it. In 1936, Archie earned a bachelor of science (BS) degree from the University of Florida.

That same year, Archie's life was about to change further. A young woman by the name of Marjorie caught his eye. Marjorie was a student at the Florida State College for Women.[2] Like Archie, she was also studying to become a zoologist. She, too, dreamed of working with animals in their natural surroundings. She once said, "My aim is to become a zoologist. I wanted to work with whole, live animals, preferably birds, in their natural surroundings."[3]

One day a group of sick quail showed up at her school. Marjorie was very worried about these sick birds. She knew she needed advice on how to help them stay alive. At that time, Archie was employed as a wildlife technician at a fish hatchery nearby. So Marjorie put the sick quail in a box and took them over to a nearby fish hatchery. She hoped somebody there would give her advice on how to care for them.[4]

Marjorie got more than she bargained for. At that time, Archie was employed as a wildlife technician at the fish hatchery. Majorie not only got the instructions on how to care for the sick quail, but she also fell in love with Archie Carr. The two became inseparable. They married the following year in 1937, the same year that Archie earned his PhD.[5] He was the first student to earn a doctorate in zoology at the University of Florida.[6] A doctorate is one of the highest earned degrees given out by a school. Marjorie also earned her degree—a master's degree (MA) in zoology.

Marjorie and Archie would go on to have five children—four boys and one girl. All four of their sons followed careers in conservation biology. Their daughter became a professional actress.[7]

Archie Carr the Teacher

After earning his doctorate in 1937,[8] Archie Carr became a professor at the University of Florida. He was an extremely popular teacher. Some students even unknowingly copied his bent arm stance. Students vied for a spot in one of his classes, which often took place outdoors. He took his students on field trips around northern Florida and southern Georgia. These field trips often took place at a swamp and in a canoe.[9]

Archie Carr's lectures were captivating, and his stories were fascinating. His field trips were always made into memorable experiences. Because of his vast knowledge, his travels, and his ability with language, he was able to create vivid pictures for his students. He could paint a picture of landscapes he had visited, animals he had encountered, sights he had seen, and the people he had met. He could even recite stories back to his students in different languages. Carr's ability with words let him take his students on the journey with him.

Archie Carr was also very funny, and he had a great sense of humor.[10] Any stories about him today usually tell of something funny he did or a prank he pulled. For example, during a class, Archie Carr wanted to get a reaction from a student. As a joke, he gobbled up a freshly caught species of fish.[11]

Other times he would wave a treacherous snake about.[12] He thought it was hilarious when he saw his students' horrified reactions.

Thomas Barbour

Thomas Barbour was an eminent zoologist in Massachusetts. Born in 1884, he had earned his PhD in zoology in 1913 from Harvard University in Massachusetts. His interests were very similar to those of Archie Carr's interests. Barbour traveled all around the world studying new animals. He was the director at Harvard's Museum of Comparative Zoology, in Cambridge, Massachusetts.

Barbour's family had a lot of money.[13] Some of this money he put toward the museum and its collection. But he also used some of his family's money to fund the promising work of young biologists. Archie Carr was one of them.

Thomas Barbour examines a bone.

Carr wrote to, Barbour about visiting the unique collection at the museum. Barbour knew all about Carr. In fact, he not only welcomed Carr, he offered to pay for his trip to the museum. After that first summer in 1937, Archie Carr became the main recipient of any funding from Barbour.[14]

Although the funds weren't large amounts, they allowed Archie to grow professionally as a biologist. Archie spent the summers from 1937 to 1943 with Thomas Barbour. Barbour liked to encourage Archie and they became close friends. Barbour sometimes would visit the Carr family as well. Barbour soon became the most important person in Archie's beginning years as a biologist. His encouragement helped Archie grow as a biologist.[15] And in turn, growing as a biologist would eventually lead Archie Carr on a quest to save marine turtles.

Barbour loved life. He was amazed by nature. He believed that people should find glory in the natural world and enjoy the natural things around them. This enthusiasm helped Carr enjoy the natural world even more than he had. Barbour's love of nature was such that when he was too old to properly enjoy it, he actually mourned it. Archie Carr's wife once noted that she saw the elderly Barbour outside one night. He was crying because he could no longer hear the beautiful summer sounds of crickets and tree frogs.

An exciting thing happened to Archie Carr in 1939. It was a spring day in May when a colleague brought a salamander to Carr. The colleague's name was H. K. Wallace. Carr was excited when he saw the salamander because it was unlike anything he had ever seen before. The salamander was white and it was blind! It was found in a two-hundred-foot well in Albany, Georgia. Archie was thrilled. He was absolutely positive that this species had not been described by anyone. This meant that nobody had recorded its existence![16]

Carr immediately wrote to Barbour to tell him about the salamander. He also hoped for Barbour to advise him. Carr was concerned because he knew that to write a thorough report, he would have to dissect the salamander. To dissect the salamander he would have to kill it. How could he do this to something as unique as this species of salamander?

An idea came to Carr. His brother, Thomas, had just received his degree in physics. He knew how to work an X-ray machine. So Carr asked his brother if they could take an X-ray of the salamander. This would allow them to see inside the salamander without harming the creature. It was a perfect solution![17]

Unfortunately, this idea did not have a happy ending. During the X-ray, the salamander fell off the table and died. After all Carr's concern, it had

⬆ *Salamander Haideotriton*

died anyway! Archie Carr decided to name the salamander after H. K. Wallace, the man who had brought it to him. He named the salamander *Haideotriton wallacei.*

🍃 Archie as an Author

Archie Carr's love of English became a gift to him in later years.[18] He was able to combine his two passions: language and biology. He wrote many science papers and published many books in his life. In 1952, he wrote a handbook about turtles. It was published by Cornell University Press. It was titled *The Handbook of Turtles: The Turtles of the United States, Canada and Baja California.*

Today, this book is still in print! This book not only stayed in print, it was an award winner, too. It won the Daniel Giraud Elliott Medal of the National Academy of Sciences.[19]

Archie Carr also wrote another book, *The Windward Road,* which he dedicated to his good friend and colleague, Thomas Barbour. This book was published in 1956 by a publishing company named Knopf. It won an award, too. A chapter from this book won an O. Henry Award (Best Short Stories of 1956). The chapter was called *The Black Beach.* Carr earned many other awards for his writing. They included the John Burroughs Medal of the American Museum of Natural History. This award was granted for his nature articles. Archie Carr went on to write more than ten books, including *High Jungles and Low* published by the University of Florida Press in 1953. Time-Life Books started a series of natural history books on continents. They called up Archie Carr and gave him his choice of which continent to write about. He chose to write on Africa.

Archie Carr also wrote more than 120 scientific papers[20] and magazine articles. Other awards he earned include the World Wildlife Fund's Gold Medal, the Smithsonian Institution's Edward W. Browning Award, the New York Zoological Society's Gold Medal, and the Hal Borland Award of the National Audubon Society. Another honor

🜂 Archie Carr on a collecting trip in 1932.

included Prince Bernhard of the Netherlands appointing Carr as an officer of the Order of the Golden Ark. Archie Carr's achievements seem endless.

His Travels

Archie Carr traveled throughout his life as a research and consulting biologist. People from other countries would ask him to help them with their studies. One year, he took a leave from teaching at the University of Florida.

In 1945, he traveled to Honduras. There, he taught biology at the Wilson Popenoe's Escuela Agricola Panamericana (Pan-American Agricultural College). This course was taught entirely in the Spanish language. Carr remained in Honduras for

Archie Carr observes turtle hatchlings in 1961.

four years. While he was there, he learned about the people of Central America. He also learned about their forests and their living creatures. In the late 1950s, he taught at the University of Costa Rica. His early years speaking Spanish with his Cuban roommate had paid off.

In 1960, Carr was part of a study that focused on marine turtle migration and navigation. This research project studied where turtles travel after they are born. This research also determined where they return to in later years.[21]

Archie Carr received a grant from the Office of Naval Research. This enabled him to fly by U.S. military transportation anywhere in the world free of charge. He flew all over the Gulf of Mexico, the Caribbean, northeastern South America, Pacific Central America, east Africa, New Caledonia, Papua New Guinea, Australia, and many other places. A colleague named Dr. David Enrenfeld later wrote a brief biography on Archie Carr. He is quoted as saying that through Carr's travels and research "his knowledge of world ecosystems was legendary." [22]

Archie and Marjorie Carr made their home in Florida. Wewa Pond, a pond filled with turtles, frogs, and other wildlife, was in their backyard. A forest was within walking distance. Although he took a leave from the University of Florida, Archie Carr remained on the faculty as a professor there

Governor Claude Kirk presents an award to Majorie Carr while her husband Dr. Archie Carr looks on. Majorie Carr received recognition for her efforts with Florida Defenders of the Environment in October, 1970.

for more than thirty years. Eventually he was awarded the title of Graduate Research Professor. This was a great honor. Carr also supported his wife's work as a zoologist. She was active with Florida's conservation. Archie joined his wife in many of her conservation efforts.[23]

Carr died of cancer in 1987. Years after his death, Majorie Carr compiled some of her husband's writings together. She produced a book called *A Naturalist in Florida: A Celebration in Eden.* Several years later, a popular television station (PBS) produced an hour-long show based on this book. It showed Carr's dedication of more than fifty-five years to sea turtles until his death.

3

The Life Cycle of a Turtle

Archie Carr had many up-close experiences of watching a turtle make her nest. Carr witnessed many female turtles laying their eggs as well. To see it as it happens, is an amazing and fascinating experience. Today, there are a number of organizations that will take you on a guided night walk to watch a turtle nesting. For those who are not able to see this happen, here is a description of how it is done.

The Making of a Nest

The beginning of the life cycle starts with a female turtle making a nest for the eggs she will lay. All

⬆ On the loggerhead sea turtle the pattern of scutes, or plates between the eyes, distinguishes species.

turtles lay their eggs in a nest. It is not a nest like a bird's nest. A turtle's nest is dugged out of the sand. A female loggerhead turtle, for example, will be ready to nest between two and twenty-five years of age. The female loggerhead turtle will appear on the beach at night. She will choose a spot that is high enough to protect her nest from the incoming tide.[1]

Once the site is chosen, the female loggerhead will begin to dig. She will use her front flippers to push the sand away. First, she digs a pit large enough for her body. The pit will allow her to conceal herself from predators while she lays her eggs.

Next, she will use her rear flippers to dig another pit. This pit is for her eggs and will become the nest. It will be two feet deep. In this nest, the female loggerhead will lay about one hundred eggs. This is called a clutch. The clutch may vary from 70 to 150 eggs. The eggs are roughly the size and shape of Ping-Pong® balls and are soft in texture. This soft texture prevents the eggs from breaking when the female drops them into the nest as she lays them.

⬆ Research excavation of a loggerhead sea turtle nest on a sandy Florida beach. The excavation is part of a county research program that keeps track of the number of nests, mostly loggerhead.

Once all the eggs are laid, the turtle hides the nest. She fills the nest in with more sand. Using her rear flippers, she whisks sand over the eggs. The eggs will be packed firmly with sand in the nest. If all goes well, the eggs will remain in the nest for up to two months. The female doesn't stop there. She will use her front flippers to disguise the nest even further. She will use them to flick sand loosely over the nest. She will also toss and turn over the nest to move the sand around. This will make it less noticeable than a fresh packed sand area. After the nest is disguised, the turtle will leave the beach. Her job is done. She will not return to that nest. She may have up to seven more nests in that season along the same beach. They will all be made the same way.

The Eggs Are Hatched

If the eggs are kept safely in the nest, they will hatch within two months. Baby turtles are born during the night when the sand temperature is nice and cool for them. Hatchlings, or baby turtles, instinctively emerge at night to avoid predators. They also want to avoid the hot daytime sun. Here is an interesting fact about what conditions determine the sex of a hatchling: Eggs that are located in warmer temperatures toward the top of the nest often become female turtles. Eggs that are at the bottom of a nest are in cooler

⬆ Loggerhead turtle hatchlings crawl across the beach.

temperatures. They will often result in male turtles being born.[2]

Once a baby turtle is out of its nest, it instinctively travels toward bright lights. Typically, it will follow the moon or the horizon over the water.[3] This will lead it safely into the ocean. However, only one in one thousand hatchlings will make it to the water safely.

The hatchlings face predators and can get confused by artificial lights that can lead them away from water. The ones that make it safely to the ocean will dive to the bottom of the water. They will let the undertow pull them out. Then they will swim for twenty-four hours without stopping. Eventually, they will reach warmer waters where two different currents meet. In Florida, this would be to the warm waters of the Gulf Stream. Archie Carr wondered about this part for over thirty years.[4]

In the warmer waters, the turtles will spend up to ten years floating on sargassum, or olive brown seaweed, before they return to nest on beaches. They will return to the coast as juvenile turtles. Male turtles will not leave the sea, though. Females will only come to shore to lay their eggs. The females often return to the same beach where they were born. There they will make nests of their own and lay their eggs.

4

The Endangered List

Archie Carr spent his entire life studying marine turtles. His studies focused mainly on seven species of these turtles. These species are found all around the world. Five of the seven marine turtles are found mainly in tropical or subtropical waters. The two other species are found mostly in the Gulf of Mexico.

Six of the seven species are endangered. This means that their continued existence is threatened. Archie Carr's lifelong study and research has brought awareness throughout the world for the need for international conservation practices to protect the future of marine turtles. These include the loggerhead turtle, leatherback turtle, hawksbill turtle, green turtle, Kemp's ridley turtle, olive ridley turtle, and the flatback turtle.[1]

The Loggerhead Turtle

The loggerhead turtle is the most common sea turtle in Florida. One-third of the world's total population of loggerhead turtles is found on Florida beaches.[2] The loggerhead turtle was named for the size of its large head. Adults can weigh 200 to 350 pounds (91 to 159 kilograms). They can also reach lengths of 3 feet (9 meters)!

An adult loggerhead's outer shell, or carapace, is reddish brown. The underbelly of a turtle is called the plastron. This part on a loggerhead turtle is usually yellow. The average length of a loggerhead turtle shell is about 36 inches (92 centimeters). A loggerhead turtle usually weighs about 250 pounds (113 kilograms).

All baby turtles are called hatchlings. The hatchlings are usually light to dark brown in color. In the southeastern areas of the United States, there are about fifty thousand to seventy thousand loggerhead nests.[3] This is about 35 to 40 percent of the entire world population of loggerhead nests.

Loggerhead hatchlings float around in rafts of sargassum, a type of seaweed. They will also float on garbage. They float around for many years. This time is called the "lost years." This is a term

A loggerhead turtle lies on the beach.

given to the years between a hatchling's birth and when it returns to coastal waters as a juvenile turtle. During these years, a hatchling grows about 15 to 20 inches (40 to 50 centimeters) in length.

Nobody knows where the majority of these hatchling turtles spend their early years. Scientists aren't even sure how long they are away. It is estimated that the hatchlings' early years last from three to seven years, but nobody knows for sure. As a young turtle, a hatchling will move to shallow coastal waters.

Adult loggerhead turtles choose a variety of nesting areas. Some live in the muddy bottoms of bays in the northern Gulf Coast. Others choose to live in the clear waters of the Bahamas. Both environments are vastly different. Nobody knows why loggerheads choose two completely different habitats.[4]

The loggerhead turtle eats mollusks, crabs, sea grass, and other small animals that are attached to reefs and rocks. They use their powerful jaws to chew.[5] Sometimes they will eat fish, but they are not really considered fish eaters.

Mating season is from late March to early June. Males wait in the coastal waters for females. The females nest from late April until early September. About fourteen thousand females nest in the southeastern United States per year. The average size of a loggerhead's clutch or a nest of eggs, is

🔆 Sea grass provides sea turtles with some of their diet.

from 100 to 126 eggs. The loggerhead female turtle nests at night. Once the eggs are laid, the female will hide the nest and return to the water. The eggs hatch between fifty-three and sixty-eight days, depending on the area and the temperature. Hatchlings are about 2 inches (5 centimeters) long.

Loggerhead turtles are threatened by many different things. In Florida, drowning from shrimp trawl nets, habitat loss, and beach lighting are their major threats.

The Leatherback Turtle

The leatherback is the largest living turtle in the world. It travels the farthest and dives the deepest in water. The leatherback travels into the coldest waters as well. The leatherback's shell is very distinctive from the shells of other turtles. It was named because of its smooth, rubbery-type shell.[6] All other turtles have bony hard plates on their shells. The leatherback's shell is flexible in texture.

Leatherbacks' front flippers are also longer than the flippers of any other sea turtle.[7] Their flippers can reach 106 inches (270 centimeters). An adult weighs between 700 and 2,000 pounds (318 to 909 kilograms). These turtles measure from 4 to 8 feet (1 to 2.5 meters) in length. The largest recorded leatherback was found in 1988. This male weighed 2,015 pounds (916 kilograms)![8] It was found stranded on the west coast of Wales.

Leatherback hatchlings look mostly black. White outlines their flippers. They are about 2.5 inches (6.4 centimeters) in length. Leatherback turtles eat jellyfish. They are known to be able to thrive in cold water, too. They have been spotted in cold Canadian waters.[9]

Leatherbacks used to be poached for their meat. Today, however, their greatest threat is to their eggs. Fishing nets are also adding to the

⬆ Leatherback sea turtles nest occasionally on the beach at Canaveral National Seashore in Florida. The leatherback is an endangered species of sea turtle and is one of the largest in the world.

decline of leatherbacks. In 1987, shrimp nets caught about 640 leatherbacks each year. Today, regulations have made the use of a Turtle Excluder Device (TED) mandatory.[10] A TED is a grid of bars with a hole at the top or bottom of a net. Shrimp can easily pass through the grid. However, larger animals, such as turtles hit the grid bars. This then pushes them out through the opening. This device has saved the lives of many leatherbacks.

Leatherbacks often choose open beaches to nest. In Florida, they nest from April to July. The shores of these open beaches have little protection. They often have severe erosion from water or wind. Sometimes it is so severe that nests full of eggs can be lost along with the erosion of the beach. There are between 70,000 and 115,000 female leatherbacks in the world.

Poaching turtle eggs is a huge threat—even though it is illegal. Fortunately, poaching eggs to eat in Florida is not. In Puerto Rico, however, poaching is a big problem. Today, in places where poaching is a problem, some areas offer night patrols of beaches to protect turtle nests.

Like all marine turtles, leatherbacks are also threatened by artificial lighting, humans, trawls, and eating garbage. They have been known to mistake a plastic bag for jellyfish. They eat the bag and die. A study showed that over a ten-year

⊙Turtle excluder device

⊙A loggerhead turtle escapes a net equipped with a turtle excluder device (TED).

period, ten out of thirty-three leatherbacks found washed ashore had died from eating plastics.[11]

The Hawksbill Turtle

The hawksbill turtle has many characteristics that differ from other marine turtles. It has two claws on each flipper. Its head sharpens to a point with a V-shaped jaw.[12] Its mouth looks like a bird's beak.[13] This is how the hawksbill got its name. It also has thick overlapping scutes on its shell. Scutes are similar to scales. The outer shell of the hawksbill is heart shaped on a young turtle. As it grows to adulthood, the shell lengthens and changes shape. The sides and back areas of a hawksbill's shell are serrated like the edge of a knife.[14] Beautiful patterns of streaking brown and black on an amber background decorate their shell.[15]

The hawksbill is an average-sized turtle. Females are about 34 inches (87 centimeters) in length. They weigh up to 176 pounds (80 kilograms) in the Caribbean. Archie Carr discovered a hawksbill turtle in 1952 that weighed a record 279 pounds (127 kilograms)! Hatchlings are about 1.6 inches (4 centimeters) in length. They weigh roughly the same as thirteen to nineteen candy Smarties®—0.5 to 0.7 ounces (13.5 to 19.5 grams)!

⬆ Hawksbill turtle swimming

Hawksbills choose different habitats for different stages in life. For example, hatchlings are believed to take shelter along weeds in the Gulf of Mexico. Just like other marine turtles, they float around on sargassum and garbage. Styrofoam®, tar balls, and plastic are often found in tiny hawksbills. When they reach a length between 8 to 10 inches (20 to 25 centimeters), they will swim back to coastal water. They make their homes along coral reefs for many years. They eat sponges found on the reefs. They rest and bask in the sun on the reefs.

When the hawsbills are ready to nest, they choose beaches in tropical areas around the world. Green turtles are often found nesting on the same beaches as hawksbills. Hawksbills' nests are often found under vegetation. They nest from July to October. They lay about four nests a season—every fourteen days. Their clutch size is about 140 eggs and takes about sixty days to hatch.

Hawksbills face the same threats as all marine turtles. However, their biggest threat is from humans. These turtles have beautiful shells. They are often killed for their shells alone.[16] This is called bekko.[17] Bekko is a Japanese term that means the shell of the hawksbill. The English term is tortoise shell. Japan is a major consumer of bekko.[18] Some people farm hawksbill turtles just for their shells. The shells are made into cabinets, hand mirrors, and cribbage sets.

The Green Turtle

The green sea turtle is found throughout the world in warm ocean waters. It is the most valuable of all the turtles. Green sea turtles are hunted for their skin, eggs, meat, and their shells. An average female will lay about eighteen hundred eggs in her life. Only four hundred of these might actually hatch. Only a little more than half of that number will actually make it safely out to sea. From here, only thirty will survive the first week in the water. This is why Archie Carr felt it is so important to protect turtles.

The green turtle is a hard-shelled turtle. Adults can reach up to 39 inches (100 centimeters) in length and about 330 pounds (150 kilograms) in weight. Hatchlings weigh about the same as twenty-five candy Smarties® or almost 1 ounce (25 grams). They are about 2.2 inches (5.6 centimeters) long.

Green turtles are white underneath their shells and black on top. This changes as they grow. Green turtles grow extremely slowly. In fact, in the southern Bahamas a green sea turtle took seventeen years to grow from 12 to 29 inches (30 to 75 centimeters)! When they dive, a green turtle can reduce its heart rate to one beat every nine

⬡ Green sea turtle swimming in the waters of the Northern Hawaiian Islands

minutes! They can also stay underwater for up to five hours on one breath!

Females usually make their nests on islands. They choose this location so they can dig a deep nest. On an island, the nest can be high above the waterline. Sometimes, a green sea turtle may travel over 621 miles (1,000 kilometers) to reach its ideal nesting site! Females lay their eggs at night. Up to seven clutches can be laid down at twelve—to fourteen day intervals. The average clutch size is around 110 to 115 eggs.[19] Females usually lay every two, three, or four years between each season.

The hatchlings leave the beach and go into the ocean after hatching. Again, nobody knows how long they spend out there. When they reach a length of 8 to 10 inches (20 to 25 centimeters), they travel to feeding areas. This is usually among weeds, sea grasses, algae, or also coral reefs and rocky bottoms.[20] Here they feed on sea grasses and algae. Predators and beach erosion account for many destroyed nests. Tumors are also a major threat to surviving green sea turtles.[21]

The Kemp's Ridley Turtle

The Kemp's ridley turtle is the most endangered marine turtle of all species. It was named after a fisherman named Richard M. Kemp.[22] Like Carr, Kemp loved nature. He sent a turtle specimen

⬆ A Kemp's ridley digging her nest

from Florida, which would later be named the Kemp's ridley. The Kemp's ridley turtle was once threatened mostly by poachers and predators. Today, however, their main threat is shrimp trawlers. There are only about twelve hundred breeding females in the world. Each one of these caught in a net is a huge loss to the marine world.

The Kemp's ridley one had a special nesting behavior. In 1963, Archie Carr's friend, Henry Hildebrand, discovered an old movie from 1947. The movie showed lots of Kemp's ridley trutles nesting on a beach in northeastern Mexico. Hundreds and even thousand of turtles will gather offshore. In Spanish, this called an arribada. This word means the "arrival" of a large group of nesting turtles. Hildebrand and Carr made an educated guess.

They estimated that there were forty thousand Kemp's ridley females nesting in northeastern Mexico. By 1985, this was reduced to only two hundred nesting females. By the year 2000, the number had increased but only to six thousand. The arribada no longer occurs[23] It was a far cry from forty thousand, but it was a step upward. At this time, poachers and trawlers were their main enemies. Today, with Turtle Excluder Devices (TEDs) used, Kemp's ridley turtles are gaining protection.

The Kemp's ridley is the smallest known sea turtle,[24] along with its cousin, the olive ridley. Adults usually measure around 25 inches (65 centimeters) in length. They are about the same in width. They weigh around 99 pounds (45 kilograms) or less. Baby turtles are grayish black on the top and bottom of their shells. As they age, the color changes to grayish olive on the top and whitish yellow on the bottom. The Kemp's ridley feeds mostly on crabs.

They nest from April to July in Mexico. Most nesting takes place at a beach at Rancho Nueve in Mexico. Almost no other nesting from this species takes place on any other beach. As mentioned, the Kemp's ridley's greatest threats are loss of beaches and trawlers. About five hundred to five thousand of these turtles are killed, drowning in a shrimp nets each year.[25] The introduction of TEDs has saved many of these turtles. Most known nests of this species are located on a beach in Rancho Nuevo. Humans are a threat to these beaches even though most of them are protected. The two main areas where this type of turtle eats are near polluted areas. Unfortunately, oil exploration and production occurs in this area.

The Flatback Turtle

Like its name suggests, the flatback has a flat, smooth body. The edges of its carapace, or upper shell, are upturned. Its carapace is often yellowish gray or greenish gray in color. Of all the turtle species, flatback turtles stay within a limited area. They are found in northern Australia, the southern parts of Indonesia, and Papua New Guinea. They rarely leave these areas. They make their homes on coral reefs. The flatback turtle eats squid, mollusks, and sea cucumbers.[26] Adults weigh up to 198 pounds (90 kilograms). They can reach a length of 39 inches (100 centimeters).

Females nest in the tropical part of northwestern Australia at day and nightime. They nest up to four times per season. They may lay about fifty eggs each time, every thirteen to eighteen days. There are up to ten thousand nests made by females in this area each year. Their eggs are quite large in size. This makes them less threatened by predators as they are too big for some. This is one of the reasons the flatblack is the least threatened marine turtle. Another reason is the area they nest in is extremely remote.[27] This means that few other animals live in this habitat with them.

However, the flatback has its own survival threats. Occasionally, a female will be threatened by crocodiles hiding in the water. The flatback is also threatened by fishing trawls. Because the area they live in is so remote, any habitat loss would be devastating.

A flatback turtle rests on the beach on Bountiful Island in the Gulf of Carpentaria, Queensland, Australia.

The Olive Ridley Turtle

The olive ridley turtle closely resembles the Kemp's ridley turtle. They are considered cousins. The olive ridley's carapace is upturned at the edges. Like its name, it is an olive green color. Similar to its cousin, it is a small marine turtle. It can reach a length of 28 inches (71 centimeters). An adult usually weighs less than 100 pounds (45 kilograms).[28] It lives in various areas from the Antilles, the northern coast of South America, West Africa, Australia, Southeast Asia, and the Indian Ocean.[29]

The olive ridley turtle feeds on mollusks, crabs, shrimp, and lobsters. Thousands of females will lay their eggs over a period of just a few days. This can take place up to seven times a season. The olive ridley has one of the most amazing nesting habits in the world. Like the Kemp's ridley, the olive ridley nests in arribadas. One arribada in Mexico had more than one million nests.[30]

Sometimes, there are so many nests that previously laid eggs are dug back up. A female may lay on the average of 110 eggs in her nest. The eggs incubate for fifty-two to fifty-eight days. In the past, the olive ridley has been caught and sold for its meat and eggs. Some measures have been taken by local people to protect this turtle. Unfortunately, there is still a market for the turtle and it is at risk.

⬆ An olive ridley arribada in Mexico. The word *arribada* means
arrival by sea in Spanish.

The highly migratory behavior of olive ridleys makes them shared resources among many nations. Therefore, conservation efforts for olive ridley populations in one country may be jeopardized by activities in another. Protecting olive ridley sea turtles in U.S. waters is important, but not sufficient to ensure the continued existence of the species.

5

Threats of Extinction

Why were marine turtles so important to Archie Carr? Turtles have been on our planet for more than 220 million years. That is a long time. You would think there would be millions of turtles. Unfortunately this is not true. Turtles around the world are dying needlessly. Because of this, many turtle species are endangered. A species of animal that is endangered faces the risk of becoming extinct, or no longer existing.

Marine turtles face all sorts of obstacles for survival. They face poachers, predators, artificial lighting, nesting interruption, garbage, and pollution.[1] The fact of the matter is that turtles are actually getting sick because of humans. Only one out of every one thousand baby turtles makes it into adulthood. Of those that do, its main predators are human beings. But why should anyone care?

Healthy animals around the world are important to us. Healthy animals show us how healthy our land and water is. All creatures have a role in the world. Some are a source of food to others. Some creatures control food populations by eating other creatures. Some do both.

⬆ In Jobos Bay National Estuarine Research Reserve, Puerto Rico, sea turtles are occasionally seen near sea-grass meadows around coral reefs.

Marine turtles are very important in marine ecosystems. For instance, green turtles eat sea grasses, algae, and tiny animals floating on seaweed. By doing this, they are also helping maintain sea-grass beds. Without grazing, sea-grass blades would grow too tall. Then, dirt would get caught around the tall blades. In turn, the sun would not be able to penetrate the water sufficiently enough to grow healthy sea-grass bedding. Disease could grow here.

By eating the sea-grass bed, the bed becomes more productive. Sea grass is also quickly digested by turtles. As it leaves the turtle's body as waste, it puts back recycled nutrients into the water. The nutrients are very important to other marine species and plants in this ecosystem. This allows them to thrive.

Sea-grass beds also function as natural habitats for other small animals. By keeping marine turtles safe, an entire ecosystem is saved. If they disappeared, it could affect coastal and ocean ecosystems.[2] By studying marine turtles and helping to keep them well, scientists are working toward making the entire world safer for everyone.

The threat of extinction is something all marine turtles face. The thought of turtles one day not existing is an unhappy thought. There are many factors leading to the extinction of marine turtles. Unfortunately, these factors are all caused by humans or the presence of humans. Sea turtles have lived on this planet for millions of years. It has only taken one century for humans to help destroy their habitats. The various threats that today's marine turtles face include papilloma tumors, poaching, human presence, artificial lighting, commercial fisheries, environmental threats, and predators.

Fibropapilloma Tumors

A papilloma tumor is a growth that is spread by a virus. In humans, this is similar to a wart. When the tumor develops with fibrous or fiberlike materials, it is called a fibropapilloma tumor. This type of tumor was first reported in the 1930s. Since then, the occurrence of the tumors on turtles has increased. However, they did not seem like a large threat until the 1980s. By the mid-1990s, the threat was obvious.

Today, the greatest single threat to the green turtle is a fibropapilloma tumor. These lobe-shaped tumors are found on the bodies of many marine turtles. They first look like white spots on a turtle's body. They start out small and are usually found around the neck and shoulders. The tumors continue to grow up to 4 inches (10 centimeters) or more in diameter.[3] The tumors are found on the soft portions of a turtle's body. Sometimes the tumors are found in the mouth and on

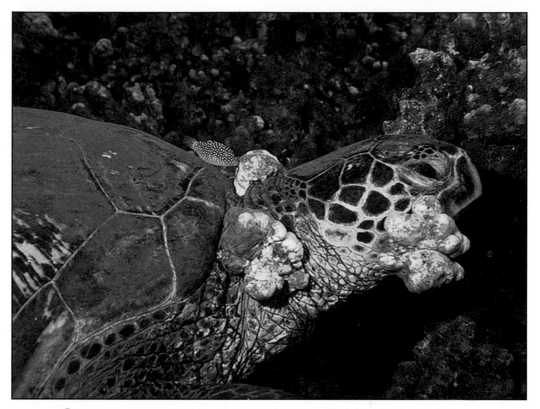

Fibropapillomas are tumors that sicken and often kill sea turtles.

the eyes. They have even been found between the scales and the inside of a turtle's body.

The green turtles that live in the Hawaiian Islands are greatly affected. Seventy percent of them suffer from these tumors. The tumors often spread. The turtles will become very ill from the growing tumors, and many will die from them. Nobody knows exactly what causes these tumors. Some believe that it is caused by a virus, but there is no known carrier. Others believe that the tumors are a result of pollution. Turtles could be stressed from pollution, making them more susceptible to the virus.[4] Pollution from the land or in the water is believed to weaken their immune systems, which fights off illnesses. A weak immune system is more likely to get infections—thus more tumors.

Nests

Every living thing needs a home that is safe. Homes nurture us and help us feel secure to grow. Turtles are no different. Turtles need a safe home to nurture their brood. They need a safe place to dig a nest and lay their eggs. A safe nest increases the survival rate of their eggs. Eggs that are protected in turn allow the turtle population to continue to grow. Unfortunately, a major threat to turtle extinction is the continuing loss of their nesting habitats. But what causes them to lose their nesting areas? The answer is simple—humans are the cause.

Turtles make their nests on sandy beaches throughout the world. Turtles aren't the only ones on the beach, though. People also use beaches for enjoyment. With the world's increasing population, the beaches are becoming crowded. Houses are built on beaches. Tourists flock to beaches to swim. A night stroll along a beach is also very common.

This has a huge impact on nesting. Turtles are sometimes scared away. This may cause them to

A sign in the sand at Florida's Hobe Sound National Wildlife Refuge warns beachgoers to tread carefully—the protected area is a sea turtle nesting beach from May to October.

change nesting sites. By changing sites, turtles might choose a more unsuitable area. These areas can be swarming with unknown predators. This can often result in a female turtle losing her entire clutch, or group, of eggs. Sometimes moving nests simply distresses a female. She may lose her entire pregnancy from the move. The population of marine turtles depends on safely hatched eggs. To hatch eggs safely, a safe nest is a must.

Besides humans, sometimes materials have a strong effect on nesting. Nests are dug deep into sandy beaches. Lounge chairs, umbrellas, or beach balls can damage existing nests. A lounge chair leg can carve into the hidden nest, crushing the eggs. A small boat may glide onto the beach to dock. It might slide right over a nest of eggs. The nest can be damaged or destroyed. Traffic from all-terrain vehicles can compact the sand on the beach. This makes it almost impossible for a turtle to dig a nest. It can also make it difficult for a newborn turtle to dig itself back out.

Beach Erosion

Turtles need to live in their natural habitats to thrive. They are not prepared to live in environments changed by humans. The turtles need to be able to nest peacefully and undisturbed on a thick sandy beach. Unfortunately, beach erosion is another cause of habitat loss. Erosion means to wear away or reduce something in size. Erosion can be caused by wind or water. Wind can blow crucial sand away making the beach smaller. Rain water or ocean water can also erode the beach by washing it away, resulting in the loss of a nesting area.

Some people have tried to help prevent beach erosion. Sometimes, however, it can seem like a losing battle. Tons of sand can be brought in to rebuild beaches. But the wind and weather blow it away again. For instance, in 2008, tropical storm Fay resulted in a loss of about 20 percent of the total turtle nests for the season in Florida.[5] The beach was washed away and so were the nests.

Even bringing in more sand to build up a beach can cause harm to a turtle's natural habitat. Sometimes, nests are buried deeper through this process. The nests might be buried so deep that the hatchlings cannot dig themselves back out. Other times, the machinery used to bring in sand changes the quality of the beach. Heavy equipment can pack down the sand into a rocklike surface. This makes it difficult for the turtles to dig their nests properly. Or sometimes this new sand may heat up too much or pack differently than the natural beach, making poor nests. It may result in turtles choosing another location for their nests, one that may not be ideal.

Poaching

Poaching means to take something that you are not supposed to take. It is against the law. People will poach something because it is worth money. Turtle eggs are highly sought after and, as a result, are often poached.

There are many uses for turtle eggs. People eat them, cook with them, and they sell them. Turtle eggs are said to be better to cook with than chicken eggs. Stolen turtle eggs across the world are a common occurrence. This has endangered the entire population of marine turtles. It is estimated that thirty thousand green turtles are poached each year from Baja, California. More than fifty thousand turtles are poached in Southeast Asia and the South Pacific. Think of how many turtles are lost from poaching! Poaching must be controlled. If not, the threat of extinction is inevitable.

Artificial Lighting

Baby turtles are very instinctive. As soon as they are hatched, they begin to dig themselves out of the nest. Instinctively, they know to head straight to water. As a guide, they follow the light that reflects off the ocean waters—the horizon or the moon. For millions of years, this has led the baby turtles safely to water. That is until humans began crowding the planet. Humans sometimes change this path unknowingly. Humans build all over beaches and near beaches. They build large buildings, waterfront homes, and put up street lamps for a stroll in the dark. At night, cars race along beach roads. What do all these things have in common? They all have lights.

This type of lighting is called artificial lighting. It is not a natural source of light, such as the moon. But baby turtles do not know that this isn't the right light to follow. They just know that they should follow light—any light. By following artificial lights, baby turtles are led right into harm's way away from the water. By following these lights, they often become disorientated. They do not know where they are. Sometimes a light will lead them onto a road. They may travel straight into traffic. Other times, they may travel right into the sight of a predator.

Some turtles become so lost that they cannot return to the water. They will die from the heat of the sun. They can not be out of water for too long a period. Even adult turtles are affected by artificial lighting. Instead of returning to the water after they lay their eggs, they move inland. This is a mistake puts them in harm's way, too. Sometimes females will avoid a safe nesting area because of the bright lights of a waterfront home. Instead, they may choose a less suitable area to make their nests.

A U. S. Fish and Wildlife Service employee tags an endangered Loggerhead turtle. The populations of this threatened species declined due to capture in shrimp trawls, loss of habitat due to coastal development, artifical light on coasts causing disorinetation of nesting females, and beach sand mining.

Predators

Turtles can lay more than one hundred eggs at a time. This can also take place several times a year. One of the most common threats to turtle eggs are predators. A predator can be any animal that feeds off turtle eggs. Predators are smart. They quietly watch an adult turtle for signs that she is nesting. As soon as a nest is made and covered with sand, the predator moves in. A predator can devour an entire nest of eggs in one swoop. Common predators include racoons, foxes, and seagulls.

Even family dogs can be a threat to marine turtles. They may roam beaches unattended and dig for turtle eggs. Raccoons are particularly destructive predators. They have been known to destroy 90 percent of all nests on one beach! Even when they are hatched, the baby turtles are still at risk. As their little bodies scuffle along to reach water, predators can catch them. Seagulls, raccoons, and foxes can easily pounce on them, scooping them up in a flash. If the hatchlings make it safely into the water, the battle is still not over. There is a risk of a shark attack. Humans can also be considered predators. Poachers steal turtle eggs to sell or eat. Fishermen catch turtles for their delicate-tasting meat.

Commercial Fisheries

Commercial fishing is a huge cause of turtle population decline. Commercial fishing is when large amounts of fish are caught for profit. Many people in some areas of the world still hunt for turtles in oceans. They collect them as they would fish. The turtles that they catch are then sold for money. A turtle is bought for many reasons. Their meat is used for food. The meat is often sold for people to use in soups. The shells from turtles are sold as well. Humans use turtle shells as decoration. Skilled craftsmen use the shells to decorate mirrors or make combs.

Sometimes people kill turtles simply to sell as souvenirs. They stuff the turtles and sell them in local markets to tourists. Hunting turtles is often banned in many areas. This means it is illegal to hunt them. Unfortunately, if people disobey the laws, this does not make them any safer from harm.

Large ships travel deep out into the ocean to fish for shrimp. However, they often mistakenly trap turtles as well. They use trawlers to scrape the bottom of the sea to gather shrimp. A trawler is like a giant net that scoops up shrimp. Unfortunately, turtles often get trapped in the trawlers. Turtles can survive in a net for only a short period of time. If they are not freed quickly, they cannot breathe. They will drown. Most often it is too late.

◑ Longlines are fishing lines that stretch for long distances in the
ocean. Sea turtles are sometimes their unintentional catch.

Before a fisherman realizes a turtle is trapped, it has died. Hundreds of thousands of marine turtles are caught by mistake each year in nets.

Garbage

It is a well-known fact that thoughtless humans litter. They carelessly throw garbage on the ground. They toss garbage along beaches and into the water. They forget that we share this planet with other creatures—creatures that shouldn't eat garbage.

Young turtles are not aware of the risks of eating garbage. They often can't tell the difference between garbage and food they should eat. They will snack on floating garbage or plastic that resembles jellyfish. Ingesting plastic into their bodies is very harmful. It is toxic. Plastic is made from chemicals that are harmful to the body. Also, swallowed plastic can plug a turtle's stomach. Then, when it eats real food, it will not get any nutrition from the food. The plastic will prevent the nutrients from entering the turtle's system. Lacking proper nutrition will eventually kill the turtle.

Oil and Gas

Sometimes oil and gas reserves are located offshore. These reserves hold oil and gas in them. The reserves pose a terrible threat to all marine life, including turtles. If there is an oil spill, people dredge the area. Dredging is a process that scrapes the bottom of the ocean. It is used to scoop up spilled oil. The process alone can destroy various habitats. It can also injure or kill populations of sea turtles.

Besides dredging, the effect of the spilled gas or oil is disastrous. These poisonous chemicals leaking into the water have a serious affect on all marine turtles—on all marine life. The oil pools on the skin and shells of turtles. Oil can affect their

⟳When we allow our beaches to become dumping grounds, we hurt ourselves as well as marine wildlife.

breathing and harm them. Tar from the oil in the water can form into balls. These are called tar pellets or tar balls. Turtles will eat them.[4] The oil globs act like glue and lock a turtle's jaws together. As quoted in his book *So Excellent a Fishe,* Carr writes: "They bite these things, their jaws get glued together and they die."[5]

6

Archie Carr's Legacy

Archie Carr tried to learn everything he could about marine turtles. He educated others about them. He made people aware of the plight of marine turtles. The many organizations that left behind or were created because of him are continuing his hard work. So, even after his death, he has continued taking care of the many species of marine turtles. With his efforts and leadership to guide them as their inspiration—the plight of the marine turtle is still recognized throughout the world even after Archie Carr's death.

Marine Turtle Specialist Group Chairman

Carr was never afraid to voice his opinion. If he believed in something strongly enough, he stood up for it—especially marine turtles. He was able to do this while serving as the chairman of the Marine Turtle Specialist Group. The group was founded in 1966 because of the endangered status of marine turtles. As chairman, he helped protect the sea turtle. Carr was part of the board for twenty years.

One such case that upset Carr was turtle farming. It is a method of farming that uses turtles as a means to make money. Turtle farming raises turtles like a farmer would raise cows. The turtles would be sold for their meat, shells, or any products made from turtles. Even though turtle farming was supported by U.S. regulations, Carr would not back down. The group began with only about 15 members. Today there are more than 250 members from more than eighty countries.

The Caribbean Conservation Corporation and Tortuguero National Park

Carr cofounded the Caribbean Conservation Corporation (CCC). It was created to study and help save marine turtles. It was also created to monitor marine turtles in Tortuguero, Costa Rica. At first, there were specific goals for the corporation. Its main focus was the green turtle. The CCC hoped to save the green turtle from destruction and give it a chance to repopulate itself. The CCC is the first corporation in the world dedicated entirely to preserving marine turtle populations. It was founded in 1959. Carr's wife, Marjorie, often joined him in this cause. She was also a major supporter of conservation efforts.

Carr researched turtles at the Tortuguero location. This study has been one of the longest-lasting studies of an animal population ever done. Their first effort as the CCC was monitoring turtle nesting activity at Tortuguero, Costa Rica. They tracked the number of turtles that came back to nest. They recorded these numbers and then tagged the turtles. By tagging the turtles, they hoped to monitor their travels. This would enable them to learn where the turtles went after leaving Tortuguero. More than thirty-five thousand green turtle females have been tagged there. Today, this tagging program still exists.

These studies brought attention to the area by others. So, in 1963, the Tortuguero nesting area in Costa Rica was finally protected. Official laws were in place to protect the marine turtle. In 1970, it was named the Tortuguero National Park. This park is a monument to Carr's life and his

⬆ Archie Carr boards a Navy Grumman Albatross seaplane to deliver hatchling green turtles in 1961.

thirty years of turtle conservation. Carr was the director of the CCC until his death in 1987.

Operation Green Turtle

One of Archie's Carr's amazing conservation efforts was called Operation Green Turtle.[1] It was launched by the Caribbean Conservation Corporation. The operation took place over a period of nine years beginning in 1959. Carr was using a grant that allowed him to use the U.S. Office of Naval Research and travel free of charge.[2] With this luxury, he was able to distribute more than 130,000 green turtle hatchlings and eggs. They were transported from Tortuguero, Costa Rica, to seventeen other countries around the Caribbean. The CCC wanted to remove destroyed nesting areas and reestablish them elsewhere. They hoped their efforts would help the green turtle population to increase.

During Operation Green Turtle, the turtle eggs were collected and moved to a hatchery. There they were examined and kept safe. Hatchlings were also collected. They were put into troughs. The troughs were kept under a thatched roof near the Tortuguero nesting beach. Each day, ocean water was collected and brought to the trough to help keep the hatchlings wet. Then a U.S. Navy aircraft landed on the Tortuguero River to pick up the hatchlings.[3] The tiny turtles were placed into wooden boxes for shipping. Each box was lined with plastic. A mat was also placed in the box to absorb moisture. This would keep the turtles wet while they traveled on the plane to their new home. Each box held about two hundred tiny turtles. Both the eggs and hatchlings were then redistributed. They were transported and put on remote nesting beaches around the Caribbean and the Gulf of Mexico.

In 1968, the operation came to a stop. The Vietnam War needed every aircraft they could get their hands on. The navy was no longer able to lend their planes to the cause. There was also no proof that the operation was working. There still were not many nests at Tortuguero. There was also no further proof that the relocations had improved nesting areas. But there was one main thing that happened as a result of the Operation Green Turtle project: The operation brought a major awareness to the problems of the green turtle. People started to recognize that these turtles were really in danger of becoming extinct. They began to listen.

Years later, Carr made a comment about the operation in his book, *So Excellent a Fishe.* He stated that he believed they should have transported only the eggs, not the hatchlings. The two thousand turtle eggs that were sent out had a low survival rate. This was because Carr felt the eggs were not handled properly.

Head-Starting Program

The CCC helped another program get off the ground. It was called the head-starting program.[4] Hatchlings from Tortuguero were taken to the Cayman Islands. There, they were kept in a safe facility and raised until they were a year old. The one-year-old turtles were then released back onto the beach of Tortuguero. The idea of the program was to keep the hatchlings safe during the most dangerous stage of their lives. This stage was the development from a hatchling to one-year-olds. There was only one problem with this program. The CCC had not learned that baby hatchlings had low survival rates—even at one year. Both programs, the Operation Green Turtle and the head-starting program, were good efforts. Unfortunately, there was still a lot to learn.

Carr realized that more effort should be put into protecting the beaches of Tortuguero. By protecting the beach, they would then protect the turtles. Protection of habitat and education became the primary focus of the CCC.

In 1970, the Costa Rican government and the CCC established the Tortuguero National Park.[5] It is the largest green turtle nesting site in the Western Hemisphere. By establishing the park, any

⬢ Tortuguero National Park

Archie Carr National Wildlife Refuge

further development along the coast is prevented. Having researchers and guards around the park also prevent poachers. The CCC encourages villagers to stop selling turtle meat and eggs.

The income from turtles did not have to stop, though. Instead, the CCC convinced the local people that incomes could be earned by inviting tourists to see the nesting marine turtles at the park. Everyone could earn from these amazing creatures without harming them. They explained that tourists would flock to the area for souvenirs. They would also need guides to walk them along the sandy beaches. The potential for income was endless. Today, visitors to the park can observe a turtle nesting. At night, they can walk on guided tours. Green sea turtles, leatherbacks, and hawksbill turtles still make their nests on this beach. A lucky visitor will see a turtle dig her nest and lay her eggs. The visitor might even see hatchlings rushing to the sea.

Archie Carr was very happy with the efforts of the CCC. He firmly believed that the organization had saved the Tortuguero green turtle colony.

Archie Carr National Wildlife Refuge

A few years after his death, the Archie Carr National Wildlife Refuge was founded. It is located on a 900 acre (364 hectares) parcel of land. It was established in 1991 and was named in honor of

◐ The Archie Carr National Wildlife Refuge hosts the largest concentration of nesting loggerhead sea turtles in the Western Hemisphere. Here a female returns to the ocean after laying her eggs. She is fitted with radio telemetry equipment so that her movements can be monitored, enabling scientists to gain a greater understanding of the species and develop strategies for restoring populations to healthy levels.

Archie Carr because his work on the plight of the sea turtle. It cost eighty million dollars to buy this land.[6] The state of Florida, local agencies, private conservation groups, and the Archie Carr National Wildlife Refuge all shared in the purchase cost of the land.

This large amount of money shows how expensive it is to protect turtles. Money is needed to buy land, fund research, and build facilities. Today, it is imperative that more undeveloped land is secured in this area. By doing this, it will help increase and protect the nesting habitats.

The Archie Carr Wildlife Refuge protects nesting areas. It prevents human activity near the sites. It stops humans from developing this land any further. The Archie Carr Wildlife Refuge also conducts surveys to aid in furthering people's knowledge of turtles. Anything they learn, they share with other scientists. They do this by teaching in public education programs.

The Archie Carr National Wildlife Refuge covers a 20-mile (32-kilometer) coastal area in Florida from Melbourne Beach to Wabasso Beach. Three different turtle species nest on this refuge: the loggerhead, the leatherback, and the green sea turtle. This area is the most important nesting area for loggerhead sea turtles. Twenty-five percent of all loggerhead turtles nest in this area. They deposit about twenty thousand eggs on this beach alone between April and September. Thirty-five percent of all green sea turtles nest here as well. In fact, this area is the second most important nesting beach in the world. There is an average of one thousand nests per mile along this coast.

How Can You Help?

People all around the world can help save marine turtles. You do not have to be a scientist. You don't even have to be an adult. Anyone can help save marine turtles. Any conservation effort on their behalf is one step closer to saving them. There are many different ways that you can help. Here is a list of some of the things that you can do to help protect marine turtles from one day becoming extinct:

- Educate yourself about marine turtles.
- Learn about the various foundations that are created that help to protect them.
- Avoid eating in restaurants that serve any type of turtle product—such as turtle soup, turtle eggs, or turtle meat.
- Tell others about the plight of the marine turtle— the greatest tool is passing on information.
- Do not buy things that are made from a marine turtle: souvenirs, tortoiseshells, combs, or stuffed turtles.
- Avoid areas or hotels located on former turtle nesting beaches—do not give these people your business.

- Do not disturb turtles that are nesting.
- Do not use loud noises on nesting beaches.
- Do not use bright lights when on a nesting beach at night.
- Leave turtles alone.
- Do not litter. Garbage often finds its way into oceans, and turtles will eat garbage.
- Research about marine turtles.
- Volunteer at the many wildlife refuges dedicated to marine turtles.

Marine turtles have safely existed for millions of years. But recently, humans have destroyed turtle habitats, stolen their eggs, and killed turtles for money. But all it took was one human being to care—a man who cared enough to reverse some of what other humans had started. Archie Carr dedicated his life to marine turtles and educating others about them.

He created conservation organizations. He spoke on behalf of the silent marine turtles. Because of him we know that it is important to protect their habitats. But mainly Archie Carr taught us how turtle populations can continue to grow instead of decline. Because of him, marine turtles are continuing to grow and prosper in the world today.

Every turtle egg and hatchling saved today will benefit tomorrow. We are giving the marine turtle population a chance to build more nests and survive. By building more nests, more eggs will be laid. If we protect the turtles' habitats, more hatchlings will survive. More surviving hatchlings will grow to be adults and lay more eggs. The cycle will continue and the turtle population will recover and grow.

By saving marine turtles, we are keeping a great man's work alive. Their plight is far from being over, but Archie Carr has opened many eyes. It is our job to continue to see what needs to be done.

Chronology

1909 —Born in Mobile, Alabama on June 16.

1932 —Receives Bachelor of Science degree from the University of Florida.

1933 —Recieves Master's degree from the University of Florida.

1937 —Earns Ph.D. from the University of Florida. First Ph.D. granted in biology at UF. Marries Marjorie Harris

1937 –1943 —Spends his summers with Thomas Barbour, at Harvard's Musuem of Comparitive Zoology. Barbour was the most important single person in Carr's life formative years as a biologist.

1945 –1949 —Professor, Escuela Argicola Panamerica.

1947 —First sees sea turtles in Central America.

1952 —Writes *The Handbook of Turtles: The Turtles of the United States, Canada and Baja California.*

1955 —Began turtle research station (would become Tortuguero National Park in 1970)

1956 —Carr's chapter "The Black Beach" in *The Windward Road* wins an O.Henry Award for Best Short Story.

1959 —Co-founds the Caribbean Conservation Corporation (CCC). Begins "Operation Green Turtle."

1960s —Starts and directs the U.S. Navy's "Operation Green Turtle," a project to distribute green turtle eggs and hatchlings from Tortuguero to nesting beaches around the Caribbean and Gulf of Mexico.

1967 —Writes *So Excellent A Fishe: a Natural History of Sea Turtles.*

1978 —Takes part in the Green Turtle Expedition of the R.V. Alpha Helix in the waters off Costa Rica and Nicaragua.

1979 —Participates in the first World Conference on Sea Turtle Conservation in Washington, D.C.

1987 —Dies in Florida on May 21.

Glossary

amphibian—An animal capable of living on both land and water.

arribada—Mass nesting of sea turtles.

artificial—Caused or produced by human beings.

biologist—A scientist who studies living things.

carapace—The top part of a turtle's shell.

clutch—The total group of eggs found in a turtle's nest.

colleague—Someone who is a member of your group or profession.

ecology—A branch of science that studies the relationship between living things and their environment.

ecosystem—A group of organisms and its environment that functions as an ecological unit.

erode—To wear away or reduce in size.

fibropapillomatosis—An often-fatal disease afflicting sea turtles in which tumors grow on the soft tissue, often covering eye, mouth, neck, or flippers.

hatchery—A place for hatching eggs.

horizon—The line where the earth and sky seem to meet.

immobilize—To prevent freedom of movement.

longlines—Heavy baited fishing lines with thousands of hooks that stretch for miles under the sea.

murky—Something that is dark or cloudy; not clear.

plastron—The belly or bottom part of a turtle's shell.

plight—An unfortunate, dangerous, or difficult situation.

poaching—The illegal hunting or taking of an animal or plant.

reptile—A cold-blooded, egg-laying, air-breathing animal with a backbone.

satellite telemetry—The automatic measurement and transmission of radio data from remote sources, such as space satellites, to receiving stations for reading analysis.

scutes—the plates or scales that combine to form the carapace and plastron of a turtle.

species—A group made up of individuals with similar characteristics.

turtle excluder devices (TEDs)—Mechanisms put on fishing nets that allow fish to be caught while allowing sea turtles to escape.

zoologist—A scientist who studies animals and animal life.

Chapter Notes

Introduction

1. Ursula Keuper-Bennett and Peter Bennett, "Dr. Archie Carr: Upon Whose Shoulders We All Stand," *Turtle Trax,* May 21, 2001, <http://www.turtles.org/archie.htm> (February 20, 2009).

Chapter 1 Who Is Archie Carr?

1. Dr. David Ehrenfeld, "Archie Carr Tribute," *Carribbean Conservation Corporation,* August 1987, <http://cccturtle.org/aboutccc.php?page=carr> (February 20, 2009).

2. Frederick Rowe Davis, *The Man Who Saved Sea Turtles* (New York: Oxford University Press Inc., 2007), p. 12.

3. Ehrenfeld.

4. Davis, p. 13.

5. Ehrenfeld.

6. Davis, p. 2.

7. Ibid., p. 13.

8. Ibid., p. 14.

9. Ibid., p. 11.

10. Jane E. Brody, "Archie Carr, Zoologist Dies, Devoted Career to Sea Turtles," *New York Times,* May 23, 1987, <http://query.nytimes.com/gst/fullpage.html?res=9B0DE0D A163BF930A15756C0A961948260&sec=&spon=&pagewant ed=1> (February 20, 2009).

11. Ehrenfeld.

12. Davis, p. 15.

13. Ibid., p. 16.

14. Ehrenfeld.

15. Ehrenfeld.

16. Davis, p. 17.

17. Ibid., p. 16.

18. Ibid., p. 17.

19. Ehrenfeld.

20. Davis, p. 17.

21. Brody.

22. Davis, p. 18.

23. Ibid.

Chapter 2 Student and Teacher

1. Walter J. Bock, "Zoology," *Microsoft Encarta Online Encyclopaedia,* 2008 <http://encarta.msn.com/encyclopedia_761567476/Zoology.html> (February 20, 2009).

2. Frederick Rowe Davis, *The Man Who Saved Sea Turtles* (New York: Oxford University Press Inc., 2007), p. 29.

3. Ibid.

4. Jane E. Brody, "Archie Carr, Zoologist Dies, Devoted Career to Sea Turtles," *New York Times,* May 23, 1987, <http://query.nytimes.com/gst/fullpage.html?res=9B0DE0DA163BF930A15756C0A961948260&sec=&spon=&pagewanted=1> (February 20, 2009).

5. Ibid.

6. Davis, p. 31.

7. Brody.

8. Ibid.

9. "Archie Carr," *Wikipedia the Free Encyclopaedia,* February 2009, <http://www.en.wikipedia.org/w/index.php?title=Archie/Carr&printable=yes> (February 20, 2009).

10. Dr. David Ehrenfeld, "Archie Carr Tribute," *Carribbean Conservation Corporation,* August 1987, <http://cccturtle.org/aboutccc.php?page=carr> (February 20, 2009).

11. Ibid.

12. Ibid.

13. Davis, p. 23.

14. Ibid., p. 33.

15. Ehrenfeld.

16. Davis, p. 36.

17. Ibid., p. 37.

18. Brody.

19. Ibid.

20. Ehrenfeld

21. Brody.

22. Ibid.

23. Frank Stephenson, "Majorie Harris Carr: The Alum Who Killed the Canal," *Florida State University Research in Review* <http://www.rinr.fsu.edu/issues/2007summerfall06_a.asp> (February 20, 2009).

Chapter 3 The Life Cycle of a Turtle

1. Jane E. Brody, "Archie Carr, Zoologist Dies, Devoted Career to Sea Turtles," *The New York Times,* May 23, 1987, <http://query.nytimes.com/gst/fullpage.html?res=9B0DE0D A163BF930A15756C0A961948260&sec=&spon=&pagewant ed=1> (February 20, 2009).

2. Ursula Keuper-Bennett and Peter Bennett, "Sargeant Leatherback Says. . .," *Turtle Trax,* January 24, 2004, <http://www.turtles.org/marines.htm> (February 20, 2009).

3. Ursula Keuper-Bennett and Peter Bennett, "Threats to Marine Turtles," *Turtle Trax,* February 12, 2005, <http://www .turtles.org/threats.htm> (February 20, 2009).

4. Brody.

Chapter 4 The Endangered List

1. "Seven Species of Sea Turtles," *Sea Turtle Restoration Project,* March 2003, <http://seaturtles.org/article.php?list= type&type=65> (February 20, 2009).

2. Ursula Keuper-Bennett and Peter Bennett, "Loggerhead," *Turtle Trax,* January 24, 2004, <http://www.turtles.org /loggerd.htm> (February 20, 2009).

3. Ibid.

4. Ibid.

5. "Seven Species of Sea Turtles."

6. Ursula Keuper-Bennett and Peter Bennett, "The Leatherback Turtle," *Turtle Trax,* January 24, 2004, <http://www.turtles.org/leatherd.htm> (February 20, 2009).

7. Ibid.

8. Ibid.

9. Ibid.

10. "Seven Species of Sea Turtles."

11. Ursula Keuper-Bennett and Peter Bennett, "The Leatherback Turtle."

12. Ursula Keuper-Bennett and Peter Bennett, "The Hawksbill Turtle," *Turtle Trax,* August 5, 2006, <http: //www.turtles.org/hawksd.htm> (February 20, 2009)

13. "Hawksbill Turtle," *NOAA Fisheries: Office of Protected Resources,* <http://www.nmfs.noaa.gov/pr/species/turtles /hawksbill.htm> (February 20, 2009).

14. Ursula Keuper-Bennett and Peter Bennett, "The Hawksbill Turtle."

15. "Seven Species of Sea Turtles."

16. "Hawksbill Turtle."

17. Ursula Keuper-Bennett and Peter Bennett, "Turtle Trax Glossary," *Turtle Trax,* July 29, 2006, <http://www.turtles.org /glossary.htm#bekko> (February 20, 2009).

18. Ibid

19. Ursula Keuper-Bennett and Peter Bennett, "The Atlantic Green Turtle," *Turtle Trax,* January 24, 2004, <http://www.turtles.org/atlgrnd.htm> (February 20, 2009).

20. "Green Turtle," *NOAA Fisheries: Office of Protected Resources,* <http://www.nmfs.noaa.gov/pr/species/turtles /green.htm> (February 20, 2009).

21. Ibid.

22. Ursula Keuper-Bennett and Peter Bennett, "Kemp's Ridley," *Turtle Trax,* January 24, 2004, <http://www.turtles .org/ridleyd.htm> (February 20, 2009).

23. Ibid.

24. "Kemp's Ridley," *NOAA Fisheries: Office of Protected Resources,* <http://www.nmfs.noaa.gov/pr/species/turtles /kempsridley.htm> (February 20, 2009).

25. Ursula Keuper-Bennett and Peter Bennett, "Kemp's Ridley."

26. Sea Turtle Inc, "Flatback Seaturtle," *Sea Turtles,* <http://www.seaturtleinc.com/turtles/flatback.html> (February 20, 2009).

27. Ibid.

28. "Olive Ridley," *NOAA Fisheries: Office of Protected Resources* <http://www.nmfs.noaa.gov/pr/species/turtles/ oliveridley.htm> (February 20, 2009).

29. Sea Turtle Inc, "Olive Ridley Sea Turtle," *Sea Turtles,* <http://www.seaturtleinc.com/turtles/olive.html> (February 20, 2009).

30. Ibid.

Chapter 5 Threats of Extinction

1. Archie Carr National Wildlife Refuge, "Sea Turtle Nesting in the Archie Carr Refuge," *Archie Carr National Wildlife Refuge,* October 2008, <http://www.fws.gov /archiecarr/photos/index.html> (February 20, 2009).

2. Ursula Keuper-Bennett and Peter Bennett, "The Atlantic Green Turtle," *Turtle Trax,* January 24, 2004, <http://www.turtles.org/atlgrnd.htm> (February 20, 2009).

3. Ursula Keuper-Bennett and Peter Bennett, "Threats to Marine Turtles," *Turtle Trax,* February 12, 2005, <http://turtles.org/threats.htm> (February 20, 2009).

4. Ibid.

5. Ibid.

Chapter 6 Archie Carr's Legacy

1. Peter J. Eliazar, Karen A. Bjorndal, and Alan B. Bolten, "Operation Green Turtle Revisited," *Caribbean Conservation Corporation,* 1996, <http://www.cccturtle.org/symposium presentations.php?page=eliazar-1996 > (February 20, 2009).

2. Dr. David Ehrenfeld, "Archie Carr Tribute," *Caribbean Conservation Corporation,* August 1987, <http://cccturtle.org /aboutccc.php?page=carr> > (February 20, 2009).

3. David Godfrey, "CCC Celebrates 40 Years of Sea Turtle Conservation," *CCC and Sea Turtle Survival League,* 1999, <http://www.cccturtle.org/velador/velart18.htm> (February 20, 2009).

4. Ibid.

5. Ibid.

6. Archie Carr National Wildlife Refuge, "Sea Turtle Nesting in the Archie Carr Refuge," *Archie Carr National Wildlife Refuge,* October 2008, <http://www.fws.gov /archiecarr/>(February 20, 2009).

Further Reading

Carr, Archie. *So Excellent a Fishe: A Natural History of Sea Turtles.* Garden City, N.Y.: Natural History Press, 1967.

Davis, Frederick Rowe. *The Man Who Saved Sea Turtles: Archie Carr and the Origins of Conservation Biology.* New York: Oxford University Press, Inc.: 2007.

Spotila, James R. *Sea Turtles: A Complete Guide to Their Biology, Behavior, and Conservation.* Baltimore, MD: The Johns Hopkins University Press, 2004.

Swinburne, Stephen R. *Turtle Tide: The Ways Of Sea Turtles.* Honesdale, Pa.: Boyds Mills Press, 2005

Witherington, Blair. *Sea Turtles: An Extraordinary Natural History of Some Uncommon Turtles.* St. Paul, MN: Voyageur Press, 2006.

Young, Karen Romano. *Across The Wide Ocean.* New York: Greenwillow Books, 2006

Internet Addresses

Caribbean Convervation Corporation
<http://www.cccturtle.org/adoptaturtle.php>

The Caribbean Conservation Corporation (CCC), founded by Dr. Archie Carr and others, has as its mission the protection of sea turtles and the habitats upon which they depend. CCC has chosen sea turtles as the focus of its conservation efforts in part because these ancient creatures are among the most important indicators of the health of the world's marine and coastal ecosystems. Its work has greatly improved the survival outlook for several species of sea turtles. Visit the CCC web site and find out how you can adopt a satellite-tracked turtle or name your own adopted turtle.

Archie Carr National Wildlife Refuge
<http://www.fws.gov/archiecarr>

***National Geographic* Kids—Animals Creature Feature: Leatherback Sea Turtles**
<http://kids.nationalgeographic.com/Animals/CreatureFeature/Leatherback-sea-turtle>

NOAA Fisheries Office of Protected Resources Sea Turtles: The Kids' Times
<http://www.nmfs.noaa.gov/pr/education/turtles.htm>

Index